FINDING PEACE

FINDING PEACE

ESCAPE FROM A SELF-MADE HELL

DERRICK TURNER

Copyright © Derrick Turner.

All rights reserved. No part of this book may be reproduced in any form or by any electronic or mechanical means, including information storage and retrieval systems, without permission in writing from the publisher, except by reviewers, who may quote brief passages in a review.

ISBN: 978-1-63732-220-8   (Paperback Edition)
ISBN: 978-1-63732-226-0   (Hardcover Edition)
ISBN: 978-1-63732-219-2   (E-book Edition)

Book Ordering Information

Phone Number: 315 288-7939 ext. 1000 or 347-901-4920
Email: info@globalsummithouse.com
Global Summit House
www.globalsummithouse.com

Printed in the United States of America

ACKNOWLEDGEMENTS

First, I would like to give thanks to my Lord and Savior, Jesus Christ Who is the head of my life. If it were not for his grace and mercy, none of this would have been possible. I also want to give thanks to my mother and father for giving me life, may they rest in peace. To my brother from whom I learned a great deal about being a man. To my sister for her unconditional love and support in some of the most trying times in my life, I love you. Thanks for never giving up on me and believing in me.

To my wife for her love, support and encouragement in pushing me to complete my book, thanks for all your help and prayers.

Last, but, not least, to all my friends who shared in my life some unforgettable memories. Thank you all and I pray that this story finds the peace of God that surpasses all understanding.

And a very special thanks to my niece Erricka for all of the hard work and effort she put into making my dream a reality.

"TO GOD BE THE GLORY"s

A special thanks to my pastor, Stanley Moore for his sermons that continue to keep me focus. To all my nieces and nephews for their love and forgiveness, and to my sister-in-law, Kelly, pray without ceasing.

PROLOGUE

Born and raised on Chicago's south side, I was a young boy with a dream of becoming an artist. But, little did I know, my life would become a living hell! The struggle with an alcoholic father and a co-dependent mother would destroy my chance for success and I would become a member of a notorious street gang, and the madness began. Ruthless gang chiefs became my idols. Trapped inside of a world of make believe love, trial and tribulation sends me desperately falling to my knees in hope of finding peace.

CHAPTER 1

I GREW UP IN a three bedroom apartment on the first floor of a two flat frame building in the notorious 'low-end' of Chicago's south side. My father drove trucks for a living and my mother worked at the neighborhood grocery store seven days a week full time. I attended Belle Deuts Elementary School, the local elementary school like my siblings before me. Now the school was different. Unlike the education system that produced teachers, lawyers, nurses and business men when my older brother and sister went there. It was now infested with young boys well on their way to becoming drop-outs, thieves, killers, drug addicts and everything else unacceptable in society. At seven years old I got my first chance to see violence at its peak. School was out and my summer vacation had just begun....

It was a scorching hot day in July and the sun seemed to have found its resting place on top of my head. I remember that day well because it was summer vacation, and in those days we had barrels of fun. But, that year was different. I believe this day changed the rest of my life.

My brother and my dad had gotten up early that morning to make repairs to my brother's racing car. My brother loved speed! His Candy Apple Red Dodge Charger was the most beautiful piece of machinery I had ever seen. With its wide slick tires and roaring engine, I often imagined the day I would drive it. My brother had skills, I watched him build the car from nothing. He was a hard working married man with a beautiful wife. Her frame was occupied by a smooth light-skinned complexion with an hour glass figure. Together they introduced to the world two beautiful children, Calvin and Marie.

Calvin had stayed at my house the previous night and the sound of the powerful engine had awaken us. We both jumped to our feet, neglecting to wash our face or even brush our teeth, we raced out the back door to see what they were doing.

"Good morning," they both said. My father extended his hand and passed me a note. "Go to Mrs. Wilson's store and get me a pack of cigarettes." Mrs. Wilson was an elderly lady who owned the corner store at the opposite end of my block. I hated going in that store, it seemed to have all the goodies the store my mother worked in didn't have, and I would always steal something. Besides, Mrs. Wilson was mean! She never smiled and she had a cold stare. She didn't scare me, I always got away. After I purchased my father's cigarettes, Calvin and I walked out the door and in the middle of the day… we saw the sun go down. In my neighborhood you never knew what to expect. Happiness one minute, sorrow the next.

It wasn't unusual for violence to irrupt in my neighborhood, it was something we were immune to. But, this day would be a day of reckoning for a man who put fear in the hearts of many. A man whose presence warranted the respect of all who crossed his path....

CHAPTER 2

CALVIN AND I froze on the store steps. We had heard many stories about the tall slim man that stood ten feet in front of us, his name was Johnny Hall. He was the chief of the Black Stone Rangers street gang. It was a ruthless organization that terrorized the streets of Chicago. His eyes were dark and they set deep in their sockets. His build was slender and toned. His hair was jet black and rested calmly on his shoulders. His hands were huge and powerful, and his cold stare pierced my soul.

Directly across the street from the store was Woods Tavern, a gathering place for the neighborhoods pimps, players, prostitutes and gang members. Johnny was in a heated argument with a woman name Tracie Spencer. Tracie had the baddest body in the hood. She was Johnny's top harlot. She was about 5 feet 6 inches tall with a honey brown complexion that looked sweet. Her hazel eyes were clear and bright. She had long curly hair that fell over her shoulders like a blanket and an ass that smiled at you like an upside-down heart.

"Where's my money," shouted Johnny! I just stood there, frozen as if it was a television show. I was afraid to move, I might miss something. Out of nowhere and without any warning, BAM! Johnny's powerful hand lifted from his side and slapped Tracie in one smooth movement. He hit her so hard she fell backwards like a junkie who had injected too much dope. Her body laid lifeless on the sidewalk. "GET UP HARLOT," he yelled. But she remained motionless. "Is she dead, is she dead?" Calvin whispered frantically. "I don't know, she's not moving". I replied.

Johnny reached into his pocket and pulled out a small handgun. He stood directly over Tracie pointing it at her chest in broad daylight. Before he could finish her off, the window from the apartment above Woods Tavern flung open. Out came the twin barrels of a 12 gauge Shotgun. "BOOM!".... the sun went down. It's all you heard as the buck shots from the blast ripped through the left side of Johnny's face. The powerful blast sent his body spinning like a top! Both hands clutching the hideous disfigurement, his life clinging to lost hope, he fell in the middle of the street, flopping like a fish out of water only to give into the reaper.

Johnny had died just the way he lived, by the sword. I couldn't believe it, Johnny Hall was dead, and Calvin and I saw the whole thing.

CHAPTER 3

CALVIN AND I raced home to tell what happened. Oddly, the news had beaten us there. When I entered the house I could hear my father in his bedroom loading his 12 gauge browning automatic shotgun. Each shell he inserted seemed to echo throughout the house. My father was about to take revenge. I wanted to see him in action.

The corner was swarmed with people looking at Johnny's corpse. Some faces displayed shock, while others looked as though their prayers had been answered.

My father burst through the crowd. Pulling me by the hand he yelled, "pick up Johnny's gun, pick it up now!" I looked down at Johnny's hand. His hands were so huge, the gun looked like a toy. The grip of death had locked the pistol tightly in the palm of his hand. I stood there thinking to myself, there is no way I'm going to touch a dead man. My father quickly noticed my hesitation. Shoving me aside, he reached down and began breaking Johnny's fingers one by one until the gun was freed. "Now pick it up," he shouted again! My father bolted toward the front door like fire had been attached to his ASS. He kicked in the door that lead to the upstairs apartment like federal agents raiding a drug house. By the time I made it upstairs my father had Johnny's killer tied up with a long orange cord. His eyes, nose and mouth had been duct taped. "Get over here," yelled my father! Standing by my father's side behind the doomed man, my hands shook as though I was being electrocuted. "This is where you separate the men from the boys," he said. It was in that moment, my father passed judgment and appointed me his executioner.

After witnessing the brutal slaying of Johnny Hall, I was surprised I didn't have nightmares. I guess I was too young to understand violence or even the value of life. Growing up in an atmosphere devoured with all sorts of low-life had become the norm. Packing a gun brought much respect, and I couldn't wait until the day came when I would earn my right to be feared.

Most of the young boys in my hood had already ventured into the thug-life. By the time I was in seventh grade, most of my friends had been in trouble with the police at least once. Some for petty crimes, such as, curfew and ditching school. While others had gun charges, burglaries and robberies, which lead them straight to juvenile detention centers.

It wasn't until the eighth grade that I learned the real power my father possessed. I mean, I had already seen and experienced the abuse from his alcoholism first hand. His street characteristics however were new to me. Yes, he was mean behind closed doors, but in the streets he was **RUTHLESS**. "GENERAL COCHEES" they called him. The general for the Blackstone Rangers. I was his son. It was believed automatic that I would follow in his footsteps. There wasn't a lot of discussion regarding my "options". I was reeled in……. and I feared nothing.…. Except living.

CHAPTER 4

Avery Park was where I spent most of my summer vacation. With its well-groomed lawn, huge swimming pool, baseball diamonds, basketball courts and plenty of room for other activities, it became my home away from home. A place to escape the repeated abuse caused by his alcoholism.

During this time my father spent a couple of days on the road. With My mother working all the time, the negative influence that surrounded me devoured me internally. But, it had not yet reached its full potential, nor had it began to surface. Avery Park was also the meeting place for the Mickey Cobras. A ruthless group of men in numbers reaching well into the hundreds. The M.C.'s were in total submission to a man named Mickey Caldwell. He ruled his mob with strict discipline. No one dared violate the laws he set in play. If so, sometimes the consequences would be deadly! Every Friday evening the M.C.'s would assemble at the park's basketball Court. They stood in perfect formation, giving Mickey Caldwell their full attention. The blood red colors they wore could be seen from blocks away. I never really got a chance to hear what they discussed, we were not allowed that close, and security surrounded the meeting. Guns were visible, and the men that carried them wouldn't hesitate to use them. Yet, there was something about these men that fascinated me.

Directly behind the basketball court was, "DEAD MANS ALLEY!"

The location had earned its name because of all the decomposed bodies that had been found back there. The old people in the hood often told stories about how they could hear the cries of those who had been left there for dead; and how the stained cement would reveal massive amounts of blood when it rained. The alley was about a block long, but, it seemed to stretch as far as the eyes could see. It was like a hell above ground. Filled with the souls of men who had died a violent death!

After the M.C.'s ended their meeting, we would walk the alley. We even saw some of the chalk lines that traced the bodies of some who died there. Each chalk line told a story of how they were killed. By the time summer vacation ended, "DEAD MANS ALLEY" had increased in occupancy and everybody knew the M.C.'s were responsible.

With summer vacation over, it was time to reset my agenda. I was in eight grade now, and high school would soon be knocking at my front door. But, I had to adjust my attitude. I could feel the temptation of evil trying to invade me. The guys who used to bully me in school wouldn't dare try it now. I had begun to build my reputation. The neighborhood gangs were on my heels, And I wasn't running. I warranted membership, and would soon have my way.

After 8th grade graduation, I spent the summer transitioning into sports. I had played baseball and basketball all my life, but playing for a high school was a dream come true. I was 6 feet 2 inches tall and handled a basketball like it was glued to my hands. My baseball skills were incredible.

I knew I would dominate the sport once I got to high school, but, would I be able to avoid the negative influence all around me. There was a part of me that wanted a taste of the thug life.

CHAPTER 5

At 14 years old, I had an 80 m.p.h. fastball and allowed nothing to get pass me on short-stop or third base. My father's addiction to baseball helped improve my skills. Even though he was drunk the majority of the time, he would always find time to help me improve my pitching arm. He taught me how to throw a curve ball, slider and screw ball. Don't be mistaken, I loved my father very much. My brother and he taught my nephew and I many things; such as, how to fish and hunt. We often took fishing and hunting trips. By the time I was 12 years old, my father bought me my first weapon. It was a 20 gauge pump shotgun and I loved it, Calvin also had one. Although my mother never approved of me learning how to shoot it, my father was determined to teach me how to kill.

It was 1981 and I had registered at Belle Deuts High School. Belle Deuts was infested with gangs, drugs and those who just took up space with no will to learn. The hallway walls were laced with graffiti and gang symbols.

The aroma of cigarettes, alcohol and Marijuana polluted the air. The bell would ring for class and people stood there like they had nowhere to go. The likely hood of becoming someone successful in life seemed impossible at Belle Deuts. Somehow, I would have to find a way to fit in. I was in a jungle, and the animal in me had started to surface.

The conservative vice lords had made its way from the Westside of Chicago and poured into my hood. The guys at my school had joined, leaving me no choice but to follow suit. This gave me a chance to get back at some of the guys in my hood who bullied me in grammar school. Being a member of the vice lords was like being a part of a family that had your back no matter what. The loves they displayed for one another was nothing like what I got at home. We were like a team. The truth is we all had special talents, but no one seemed to be focused on developing their craft. Being a part of the organization required a lot of my time, which I didn't mind. It gave me a chance to escape the issues I was dealing with at home.

Every Friday we would assemble at Avery Park for our meetings. We wore black and gold to mark what we represented. The colors were bright and eye catching and the girls loved our swag. Every member paid dues that would fund upcoming events; trips to Great America, picnics and summer activities. We were more like a social club, until the M.C.s got jealous. By the time the summer rolled around, we were at war!

Guns had become our best friend. Every time we met, guns were issued out to the foot soldiers. Contracts were given and carried out. Avery Park had turned into a battlefield and the "DEAD MANS ALLEY "increased" its body count! The neighborhood had become an unsafe place for the children to play. Gun shots rang out in the night, leaving the morning hours to tell the story of what happened. Mother had become over protective and insisted I be in front of the house by the time the street lights came on. To keep me out of the street, she gave me the basement and permission to invite my friends there. But, of course it came with conditions, no thugs ALLOWED!

I had no idea on how I was gonna keep the thugs out.

All of my friends were thugs and so was I, so we thought.

CHAPTER 6

M
Y MOTHER HAD planned a family cook-out the following weekend and I knew all my cousins would be there, I knew I would have to hide my new identity from my uncles and aunts, it would crush them. Besides, my mother didn't know I was affiliated and I wasn't about to let it slip.

The grill was smoking with the pleasant smell of hickory. The ribs looked so good, my mouth began to water. Cakes and pies of all sorts occupied the kitchen table, waiting to be devoured by my hunger for sweets. The refrigerator was full with ice cold beer, with the exception of a few cans my cousin and I had stolen and hid its empty contents in the bottom of the garbage can.

With-in a matter of minutes the entire backyard was full with family and friends of all ages. Adults formed a circle in the backyard comfortably in the chairs provided, and told old tales of the south. Some were true, but, most of them were lies; nevertheless, we loved listening to them. Wisdom came from those conversations and I was a sponge.

My Aunt Lucy had finally arrived with her children, Randall, Shama and Tori. Aunt Lucy took a seat next to my mom. While the rest of the kids ran wild and loose, I noticed Aunt Lucy in a secret conversation with my mother. My mother turned to face her, giving her full attention, I saw her wipe what appeared to be a tear gliding down my aunt's cheek. I was aware of my uncle Raymond and her separating; but, I thought she had gotten over it when she started dating John, her new boyfriend. John was weird. He was a tall and huge man; very quiet and unpredictable. His eyes were cold and he never blinked. It was something about his presence that disturbed me.

Most of the family began eating, but, not me. I kept my focus on Aunt Lucy. She was hiding something and I knew it. I decided to get closer to the conversation. I pulled up a chair next to my mother and I could see the bruises around my aunt's eyes that she tried to hide behind the dark glasses she wore. "Hell No, "I shouted! "Who did this auntie!" She looked at me and burst into tears.

For the next hour, she told my mother and me how John had been beating her; and how she had left him three weeks prior to the cook-out. She had moved to the Eastside of Chicago on 76 and Kingston. She kept it a secret out of fear that John would find her. My mother sent me in the house to get her a beer. While I was in the fridge stealing one for myself, the phone rang. When I answered it, I didn't recognize the voice; it was John. "Where the hell is Lucy, "he yelled. "Who is this," I responded. "It's John. You tell

Lucy I'm going to make her suffer for the rest of her life!" Before I could respond, he slammed the phone down so hard I dropped the receiver and stepped back as though I had heard the voice of Satan. I froze, thinking to myself, what could he be talking about? What had Aunt Lucy done to him? I didn't know if I should tell my aunt, it would probably mean more beatings; so, I kept it to myself.

It was getting late and the cook-out was coming to a close. Everybody had had plenty to drink and eat. Some were fixing plates to carry home, while others were finishing up the last of the spiked punch. I rushed in the house to hide me a few cans of the leftover beer while I assisted in cleaning up the mess.

For some awkward reason I couldn't get the sound of his voice out of my head.

There was something lurking in his dark statement. Something evil and sinister, but, I couldn't put my finger on it. Even though I thought he was a weird and strange man, I under estimated him and he caught my whole family off guard.

CHAPTER 7

THE NEXT DAY I got up around 6 a.m. I had to hurry so I could make it to my aunt's house in time to get the kids ready for school. I got dressed and headed for the bus stop. The Ride seemed longer than previous times, and the buses were extra crowded. I sat patiently, but, I couldn't get that disturbing phone call out of my head. It was like a broken record playing over and over in my mind. What had he meant by making my aunt suffer? I had no clue. I would soon learn the meaning of those horrible words.

The bus driver gently pulled up at my stop. I exited the bus and walked to my aunt's apartment. After climbing three flights of steps, I was at the front door. The door was slightly jarred, music was playing loud from somewhere in the apartment. I pushed the door open and an awful smell engulfed my nostrils. The front door opened to the kitchen. There was three bowls of cereal on the kitchen table. The load music had refocused me and I turned my attention in the direction of Randall's room. I found myself standing at his bedroom door. With the door slightly open, I peaked in. The far wall, the floor and the wall above his head was covered with blood. The twin size bed occupied a lifeless shape under the covers. Five feet in front of me was a nightmare waiting to unveil… I stood directly over his bed, my entire body seemed paralyzed. My brain signaled my hand to move, but… its members wouldn't respond. Snapping back to reality, I snatched the covers from the bed. What I saw was hideous! His skull had been crushed! Skull fragments and huge clots of blood claimed the place where his head once laid. The music was now visible. His small radio covered in his own blood, played beneath him.

Standing there replaying John's phone call in my head, I thought to myself, "the girls," Sherry and Tori's room was next door. Leaving one nightmare and entering another, I walked into the girls' room. The scene was identical to Randall's room. Sherry was lying face down with her legs gapped open in a y shape. Her head had been crushed and she had semen running from her vagina. Her finger nails revealed a struggle. She had massive amounts of torn skin under her nails; she had fought for her life. Tori was positioned on her back in the bed next to her sisters. Her head also crushed. The lives of three beautiful children had been snuffed out and my soul had been scared.

I don't remember what happened next, I passed out. I woke up minutes later covered in blood.

I don't know how I made it home. It seemed like the nightmare was over and I found myself sitting on my living room couch surrounded by family members. Everyone screaming questions at me about the murders. All I wanted to do is get my hands on John.

My Aunt Lucy had gotten the news at work. She was devastated. I knew she would never be the same. John had taken all three of her children and he had to pay with his life!

The next day, my neighborhood was like a ghost town. Everyone walked around like zombies. The atmosphere felt dim and lonely. The sun had lost its shine and the sky was filled with dark gloomy clouds lingering over my head. I sat on my front porch unable to focus. I kept thinking to myself; "maybe I should have told someone about the phone call." I was starting to feel responsible for what had happened to them.

Later that afternoon my mother got a call from the police. They told her they had John in custody, he had turned himself in. He told the police he entered the apartment by climbing the fire escape. He waited patiently until my aunt left for work. He climbed through the bathroom window and murdered her children.

The chiefs of all the gangs in my hood put out a contract on his life. This was not how they did things. Children were valued above everything to these men. Funny because they lived moral-less lives but held strong convictions about right and wrong. It was immediately forwarded to the members of their gang families in the county jail. That meant that no matter where Jonny went, he would not be able to hide. In the meantime, we had to prepare ourselves for the home going of three beautiful young children. My aunt had been admitted in the hospital under heavy sedation. She was placed on a twenty four hour suicide watch. I never went to see her, I knew I wouldn't be able to look at her in that condition. My mother told me every time she went to visit, Aunt Lucy just sat there mumbling her children's names, fumbling with her hands. My mom said, she bit her nails and pulled out her hair until they tied her to the bed.

For the rest of her life…..she would regret ever crossing the path that John occupied.

CHAPTER 8

Across the street from my house was Calvary Missionary Baptist Church. My aunt's kids were baptized there. Rev. Mitchell pastored the church for as long as I can remember. He was a short, partially grayed haired, round black man with beady eyes. When he wasn't in the church preaching, he spent his time walking through the hood telling people about "how good God is". He would always corner me and shake his crooked finger in my face. "God is watching You", he would say. I never responded. Somewhere deep inside my soul, I knew he was right; God was watching me and listening too. His warning made me think about the things I said about John and how I wanted to see him dead.

A week had passed since the murders and the hood's scenery hadn't changed. The sun had ceased to shine where we lived and It rained every day. Death had stolen the lives of many in my neighborhood, but none killed the spirit of love ones like the death of those three kids. I dreaded the day I would have to attend the funeral. Even though in my head I knew it was real, I knew once those precious bodies were laid out in front of everyone there would be no denying it.

The funeral was that Saturday morning. My mother woke me up at 7 a.m. Catching me in some much needed rest, she pushed my bedroom door open and said, "get up boy, it's time to start getting yourself together. The service begins at 9 a.m. and I don't want to be late." I lifted myself from the bed slowly. Somewhere in my unconscious state, I had escaped the nightmare, and they were still alive. I sat on the side of my bed letting reality bring me back to the issues at hand.

My mother had laid out my suit. Family members were arriving at my house by the minute. The house and the porch were packed with people crying in anticipation of what they were about to face. I tried to be strong, I didn't cry. I still refused to believe it. I told myself I wouldn't cry. Until I saw them lowered into the earth from which they came.

My mother and I were dressed and ready to look death in the face, at least that's what we thought.

Every parking space on my block was occupied. Cars were lined up all the way past the park three city blocks away. The family started to line up in pairs outside the church. My mother assumed her spot as matriarch in the front of the line holding my aunt close to her. She looked so pale and weak. I didn't know what it meant to say someone looked like the life was sucked out of them…. until this day. Her eyes were wide open and piercing through time and space. It was as if she saw her children in some distant place. Her legs were shaking and her hands trembled with every step she took toward the front door of the church.

Standing directly behind my mom, I could see the children's caskets lined up in an arch at the foot of the altar. We crossed the threshold of the church and it was hallowed ground. Randall's casket was to the left of the altar. Tori's casket was in the center and Sherry's casket was on the right. Randall was dressed in a charcoal grey suit with his hands to his side. Tori was wearing a pink ruffled dress that complimented the peaceful look on her face. Sherry laid peacefully, laced in a white dress with a glossy finish. The mortician's had done their best to make them look like children. The reconstruction of their faces however and the wigs… those images don't leave you.

Once the family was seated, the ushers assisted the rest of those who were in attendance. Within minutes, the church was full with people standing against the walls. Rev. Mitchell took his place at the pulpit and begin preaching the service. Just as he commenced, the Chapel doors flung open with such force, it startled everyone in the pews. It was My Uncle Raymond, the kids' father.

"No, no, no, not my babies!" he screamed. Before anyone could respond, he bolted toward the place where his children rested. Standing directly over Randall, he picked his lifeless body up out of the casket. Clutching him tightly, he walked up and down the aisle whispering something in his ear. My father stood to intervene. Pastor Mitchell stopped him. "Wait brother, It's between him and God" he shouted. Uncle Raymond held on to him as though it was his only chance to embrace God. He laid Randall down and picked up Sherry. Everybody watched him with tears in their eyes. He repeated the same journey with both the girls. No one spoke. Not a sound could be heard. It was as if the earth stood still at that moment in our world.

I sat there thinking to myself, if only I had gotten there earlier. If only I had taken him seriously. Something inside me wouldn't let me accept their death or forgive myself for not somehow preventing it. Yes bad people do bad things, but these kids didn't do nothing to nobody. They didn't deserve to be cheated out of life.

Uncle Raymond finally took his seat in the first pew next to my Aunt Lucy. She didn't have an expression, her face was blank. Her eyes were still wide open as if she saw something no one else could see. Her body was stiff, she didn't move. My mother would later tell me she was cold to the touch. Kinda' like the walking dead.

Now that things had calmed down, Pastor Mitchell began to preach. He spoke about how important it was for the father to be in the home to protect his family. He spoke about the love of God and how important it was that we acknowledge his power. He wanted us to understand God's work. "God's work?" I thought to myself. How could a loving God allow something like this to happen? He was supposed to be a God of love. Regardless of how I viewed God's work in this case, I knew not to question His will. But it would shape, change how I looked to God for a long time.

Pastor Mitchell had delivered a beautiful sermon. Now it was time to put them to rest. The ushers asked everyone to stand while they lined up the family first. After they brought out the caskets, we all headed for our cars. This was the part I didn't want to see. I knew it would mean I would never see them again.

The death of my nieces and nephew only added to the evil in me that longed to be released. Somehow, I knew if I didn't control it, mercy would never be an option. The children's deaths had shaken me to the core. What little sanity I had left was now lost. Knowing someone could be angry enough to do this to children. It made me wonder if My father was capable of such violence. After all, my mother and I had suffered abuse many times at the hand of an angry drunk. What John had done would haunt me for the rest of my life.

Death was such a harsh reality now. It made me reflect back to the times my father had physically abuse my mom and I. The many nights I sat up in the center of my bed thinking of ways to kill him There were many of times I had planned it, but, I didn't have the nerve to see it through.

But, now I had seen the evil man was capable of, the cold and chilling blood that flowed in his veins and the senseless regard he can possess for the precious gift of life, I knew only prayer would keep me.

CHAPTER 9

AFTER SUMMER VACATION passed, my sister transferred me to Hyde Park Career Academy on the eastside. She was increasingly concerned about where I was and who I was becoming in my current situation. My sister lived on a busy street but on the south east side of Chicago. Right across the street from a golf course, a short walk to the lakefront, it was like a whole different world. Her apartment lined a neighborhood filled with big houses and well off black folks. My mother decided to let me move in with her to keep me safe, even though it meant she would be left to face my father on her own. My sister was the bookworm in our family and my education would need her guidance.

Hyde Park was a huge school. It had four floors and long hallways. Unlike Belle Deuts, the walls were clean and the floors shined with a high glossy finish. The air was fresh. No cigarette smoke, no smell of weed in the bathrooms. My first week went well. I got introduced to the baseball and basketball coaches. This would be a chance for me to show of my skills in both sports. A chance to get a scholarship and hopefully play at the college level, and then pro. I had big dreams in those days, and I was determined to make some of them come true, or at least one. With the children's death still fresh in my mind, it would be hard to focus on anything positive. Somehow, I needed to find a way to move on.

Basketball tryouts came around and I made the team. Since Geoffrey Hardaway was the team's star player, I knew I couldn't hold back. And I didn't! I averaged 30 points, 10 rebounds and 13 assist per game in my sophomore year. I earned my position as strong forward and held my weight without error. Geoffrey Hardaway and I became good friends. We studied one another at every practice. It was like we had an invisible string attached to the ball that lead from my hand to his. I secured a starting position for the duration of my high school years. Don't get me wrong, Hyde Park had its share of gang members too. They were just low key. Growing up in a neighborhood devoured by gang activity gave me an eye for others who were involved. It was easy to tell who was who.

The eastside had always been known for the Stones, and Hyde Park was full of them. Most of them played sports and hung out at Jackson Park across the street from the school. Winter, Spring, Summer and Fall, it didn't matter they were there. It was only a hand full of Vice Lords at Hyde Park, so I tried hard to stay focused. Besides, living with my sister required education first and she didn't play when it came down to the books. The spring months were the best at Hyde Park. All the girls you didn't see when it was cold outside, surfaced as soon as the sun came out. Everybody would be with their own click. You had the preppy boys, with their flooding pants and suit coats with safety pins pinned down the arms. High top fades were in style back then. The preppy boys wore them with pride.

Next, you had the G.Q. boys. They sported the sharpest dress slacks and shirts. Tailored made suits and Stacy Adams dress shoes stood out in the bright sun. You would think all the girls would be smothering the G.Q. boys, but, they were more into the athletes. The basketball and football players had all the women, all except mine. I had my eyes fixed on a girl in my art class, Yvonne Nelson. She was one of the finest juniors at Hyde Park and very smart. I thought having a girlfriend would somehow keep me focused and out of trouble. I just couldn't stay away from the hood. There was something inside me like a small voice constantly calling me, reminding me of the power I could have on the streets. Power I surrendered everyday being a 'good' boy. I was just itching to put my muscle to use to make a name for myself. I didn't understand delayed gratification and I didn't care.

During the spring months I also studied the gangs at my school closely. Me being a member of the Vice Lords had gotten out and the Stones didn't like it. When I went to my parent's house on the weekends, I told my boys about the drama brewing at my school. I wanted them to be ready if anything jumped off. Even though Hyde Park wasn't a school known for gang banging, I didn't trust the Stones as an organization. I grew up around them and I knew how treacherous they could be. Most of all, I knew they hated Vice Lords. I wasn't a killer and didn't want to be one. I grew up with plenty of them. Guys whose names I won't mention. Guys I knew didn't show no mercy! I knew what to do if the situation changed.

As the sophomore year came to a close, the violence at school started to escalate. The Gangster Disciples from 63rd Street got into a turf war with the Stones on the streets. It brought the drama straight to the school's front steps. The war had nothing to do with me and mine, so, I stayed out of the way. I continued playing sports and tried to keep my grades up. My sister kept encouraging me to stick with my skills on the court and not give my attention to the negativity that surrounded me. I took her advice and got ready for my junior year. That year all the scouts from different Colleges and Universities would be looking at young players. As bad as I wanted my on the court skills to take me to the next level, I couldn't stop working on my street skills. What I represented in the hood was a bigger part of me. Plus, I couldn't just walk away. My 'family' would kill me.

The mistake was I spent my whole summer back in the hood. It felt good to be back around the guys. The hood had gotten its grip on Lil' Johnny and he had received the rank of Lieutenant for the Vice Lords in our area. Lil' Johnny and I were best friends growing up. His involvement in the mob separated us. He had lost his will to gain an education and devoted his life full-time to the streets. The gang banging escalated while I was away. Now everybody packed a gun. The hatred between the M.C.'s and the Vice

Lords was out of control. People were getting shot and killed. Houses were being burglarized without regard or respect. Guys came up missing every month. "The Dead Man's Alley" made room for new residents. The fear of death was in the air. You could feel it every morning. I was on guard and prepared myself for the unexpected.

The neighborhood wasn't the same anymore. The meetings were moved from the park in the open to Veto's house. The friends I had that didn't involve themselves in the street violence started to look at me for guidance. I believe God was in this, because I took them all under my wing. I formed a social club and we threw parties every weekend in my parent's basement. We cleaned up all the mess my father had stored in there and we spray painted the walls green. We called it, the "Under Ground."

Forming the social club was a good idea because it kept us all busy. While the gangs were running around killing one another, we were throwing parties every Friday and Saturday night. My mother didn't know I was in a gang, so, I didn't participate in a lot of the mischief. She would have killed me herself. I had all the latest records and the some of the best stereo equipment money could buy. Listening to the hot mix five on WBMX paid off, I was a beast on two 1200 technique turntables.

Our social club consisted of eight members, Tracy aka delightful, Calvin aka Ghost, Dwayne aka Doom, Steven aka Jay, James aka Crip, Leroy aka Bones, David aka MeMe, and myself aka Daylight. We had group colors, black and gold. We bought uniforms to represent our social club. We played baseball and basketball against other neighborhoods all summer. At the end of the season, everybody got trophies. We were kids that summer and I loved it!

All summer long I kept thinking about my surroundings. How was my life going to end up? My father's drinking had gotten progressively worse. He and my mother now fought all the time. I was venturing into manhood and I was fed up with his abuse. I was big enough now, and in my head bad enough, to take him. But what if he killed me? I needed someone I could talk to and God saw my need. That summer I met the person who would become my brother for life. James Taylor and his brothers had moved from the roughest housing project in the city of Chicago, Cabrini Green. The violence that swarmed the six high rise buildings that made up the base had claimed the lives of so many the area became known as "Little Vietnam."

The gang members that lived there were killers of the worse kind. Young men with no regards for life, arose to their feet every day to take the breath of one of God's children. There was no code. There were no rules. The killings made the headlines frequently, and the guys responsible seem to love the attention.

CHAPTER 10

AFTER THE SUMMER ended, I started my junior year at Hyde Park. That year a lot of students from Kenwood Career Academy transferred to Hyde Park, mostly girls. The two schools had been in competition for years on a social level. To be honest, Kenwood had us beat. They did have the finest girls, no doubt. At the beginning of the school year I still spent a lot of time in the hood. James and I we're becoming good friends. He seemed to be the coolest dude I had ever met. He was a tall skinny young man with long hair. It was something about his look that caught my attention. He had that cold stare that sent chills down your spine. That look alone earned him the right to be labeled him a thug. It was obvious he didn't take no shit.

When it came to women, James was more like the player type. He was not getting tied down or settling down. He liked moving around. I was determined to learn his game. I watched him as he moved through the girls in my neighborhood like he was invisible. They seemed to be captured by his conversation, swag and good looks. James didn't only add to the game I picked up from my father, he also taught me everything I needed to know about the real Vice Lords. He took me up north to meet the real killers! Those who lived to take a life. He knew everyone that called the shots in the mob. He was well respected and had a reputation as a leader. Our friendship gave me instant street credit.

Every weekend I hooked up with James and his two brothers, Ed and Lie Lee. We hit the clubs dressed to kill. My mother didn't care much for James. She said she didn't like the way he treated women. To me, it was fascinating to see him in action. When we walked through the doors, all eyes were on us. James and I were always the cleanest in the house. He made sure of it. James was always the life of the party. In comparison, I was kind of shy back then. Since I was under age, James would order our drinks. We would find us a table somewhere against the wall so we could see everything that moved…. Good, bad and in dresses.

The south side was always known for the Gangster Disciples. Every club on the south side was full of them. It didn't stop us from representing. We wore our flag with pride. I guess I didn't understand how serious shit could get in the streets. I had yet to experience a life and death situation. One day that would change.

I was glad James had introduced me to the guys up north because I knew one day I might need them. The guys I grew up with were killers too. They just never left the hood.

My sister tried hard to keep me in line, but I had attached myself to James. I was picking up all his bad habits. I was about 17 at the time and I had tried weed for the first time with James. I liked it. I liked the feeling of just not feeling. Everyday James and I got ourselves a fat sack of bud and a pint of Bacardi dark rum. We sat on his porch and got so high our eyes were red as fire. I didn't understand the severity of drugs, nor did I know anything about addiction. All I knew is that, I was having the best time of my life… and feeling NO pain.

Being an upper classmen also brought about a different image. I was in the big league now and I would have to step up my game. I started hanging with the wrong crowd and my grades began to decline. Girls became more important than education. Getting high every day at lunch period became the norm. Funny how trouble will find you if you're open to it.

I was slipping. Well on my way to slipping right out my sister's door too. She was having no parts of it. I had to tighten up or she was going to send me home. I could do the streets. What I could not do was that house anymore. The drinking, the cussing, the fighting… nope I wasn't going back there. It wasn't until the middle of the year that I regained focus. I met Sharon Ward, a sophomore who loved the Lord. She had a voice like Patti Labelle. She reeled me back in. Spending time with her kept me away from the negativity. Even then, God was looking out for me. Sending angels to help. I just didn't know it was Him. Every day after basketball practice I spent a lot of time with Sharon. We would catch the bus to her house and sit on her front porch. She would lay my head in her lap and sing to me. Her voice sent chills down my spine. She had a way with making me feel special. All II needed to do was win her parents heart and I did. Sharon's mother was crazy about me. Even though her father and I got along fine, he always gave me those strange looks.

Back in the hood, James was fast becoming the neighborhood "hoe". He had more girlfriends than I had underwear. We still hung out a lot and I sucked up all the game I could. Outside of what I picked up from my father, James taught me all I thought I needed to know about women. Even though he was a member of the Vice Lord Nation, he wasn't the violent type. If you asked me, he was just a player who hid behind the mob. The guys in the neighborhood didn't approve of James and his brothers because they didn't honor them. In due time all hell would break loose between the guys in my hood with James and his brothers.

James would always tell me not to trust vice lords in my hood because they were disciples first. He had been to war with them in the past many times. He had lost many friends at the hands of their guns. I started to take his advice and slowly put some distance between them and myself. My eyes started to open and it all became clear. Why was I a part of something or someone I couldn't trust?

CHAPTER 11

LIFE WAS BEGINNING to have a different effect on me. Suddenly, I wanted to grow up. I wanted to put away the foolishness and become a real man. You would think a father would be the example a boy would follow while venturing into manhood. But, not in this case, it was my mother who began to teach me what being a man was all about. She sat me down and gave me the tools. She always told me not to pattern after my father. She said Jesus was the perfect example of a man. Even though she had spoken of Christ my entire life, I must admit I never gave it much thought. Not saying I didn't believe in Christ, I just didn't know how to connect.

Although, my mother didn't raise me in the church, she was a God fearing woman. There was a picture of Jesus on our living room wall. Right between Martin Luther King, Jr. and Malcom X. We had conversations about the bible all the time. I loved talking about God, I just didn't understand the way he did things. I mean, I had seen some horrible things in my life. The God my mom talked about had all power. He was supposed to be a good God. If this was so, why were little children being found in garbage bags? Why was the concrete in the dead man's alley stained with so much of the blood from guys I knew? Why did God allow those children to be killed? I hadn't realized yet that God punishes the just and the unjust... I was about to find out. They say a hard head makes a soft behind. Man was that ever so true...

CHAPTER 12

AFTER THE SUMMER ended it was time to get back to the books. This was it, my senior year, time to get my act together for real! I was one in a few who had made it that far and there were plenty looking to see me fail. I didn't mind. I was ready to get out of the hood anyway. The devil wasn't through with me yet.

Living with my sister was better anyway. It was like I had two different people living inside me. One on the left whispering evil in my ear and one on right whispering good in that one. I only had five classes in my senior year which meant I would be out around 1: 15 p.m. every day. I had given up on sports and devoted my attention to my God given craft, art.

Although I was over whelmed that I had made it thus far, I couldn't help but think about the guys in the hood who had lost their chance at an education, at a life. I would be the first off the block to graduate high school. I spent the beginning of my senior year trying to decide which direction my life would take. Since I wouldn't be getting a shot at pro ball on any level, I really didn't know what I wanted to do or what I wanted to become. Everyone in my family thought I should pursue my natural talent, art. I loved drawing, but it wasn't what I wanted to do for the rest of my life.

Senior year was one I'll never forget…. Since most of my friends played sports, they didn't have a lot of free time after school like I did. All the players were scouting the cheerleaders, trying to decide who would be their prom date. As for me, I was single at the time and the girl I was interested in was dating the star pitcher for our varsity baseball team. Her name was Kim Peters. She had transferred from Lindblom the previous year. Kim Peters and I had become best friends in my junior year. She was about five feet tall, long wavy jet black hair, hazel eyes, light skinned with a body of a goddess.

As the senior year progressed, I got serious about my education. I didn't want to look stupid at graduation time and not be walking across the stage. There were too many people depending on me to succeed. I wanted to be the first one in my hood to prove that graduating was not an impossible task, but it was a necessary one. It was something no one could take from you.

CHAPTER 13

TOWARD THE END of the school year my grades started to decline. I got too wrapped up in hanging out with the guys instead of going to class. Somewhere I lost the desire to make my mark in the world. I was becoming just what I didn't want to be, a failure. I couldn't seem to make the right decisions anymore. The will to do wrong had taken over me, and I was losing my focus. I could see my father's ways starting to surface. I guess I was getting what I ask for, a chance to be just like him. I found a new group of thugs. Failing required little effort. Unlike getting good grades and doing well, I didn't have to work at failing. It came naturally.

We assembled everyday across the street from the school at Jackson Park. Everybody would pitch in and buy a bundle of joints. We smoked and smoked and smoked until our eyes were blood red, damn near closed. We sat in the park looking like a bunch of silly ass china men, laughing at any and everything we saw and thought of. It was crazy because, most of our teachers could see us from the classroom windows. We didn't care. We never let it stop us from partying. We met up every day at the same time, in the same spot, doing the same thing, wasting away our future. We were living for the moment, with no intentions of fulfilling any of our goals.

Prom time was approaching and I didn't have a date yet. Taking Kim Peters was out of the question. I was too shy to ask her. Besides, I didn't want to ruin a good friendship. Although she had broken up with her boyfriend, I just couldn't muster up the courage to ask her. Two weeks before the prom, Hyde Park's most attractive senior walked up to me and asked me to escort her to the prom. I was lost for words. How is it possible that the most attractive girl in school does not have a boyfriend or even a date? It took a few seconds for it to register, but I couldn't shout YES fast enough. I walked home that day ten feet off the ground. I was going to be taking the finest girl at my school to the senior prom.

On the day of the prom the weather was just right. A beautiful day in the middle of June, 1985. I was sharp as a tack! I wore a snow white tuxedo with a metallic gold copper bond and bow tie. My date had on a metallic gold and white lace dress that hung just below her knees. The prom was on a Friday night at the Hyatt Regency Grand Ball Room. My date's best friend got stood up at the last minute, so she joined us. I walked in my prom with two of the most beautiful girls at Hyde Park. When I walked in all eyes were on me and my dates. You could feel the jealousy in the room. It was so thick you could cut it with a knife. I found us a table and sat down with my legs crossed as if I was the godfather himself. My mind was so far away from the prom. All I could think about was, "damn, I made it, against all odds, I made it!" Now, what's next?

After the prom ended, we were so drunk we didn't even attempt to go to the after party. We found us a hotel and checked in. The next morning, we woke up not knowing how the hell we got there. The room was in shambles as we stirred around looking for our clothes, trying to figure out if we had had sex. No one seemed to remember. It was Saturday morning. We needed to get ready for the senior picnic at the forest preserve. All I could think about was, "damn, I spent the night with two of the finest girls at my school and I don't even remember what happened, if anything did happen."

By the time we reached the picnic, it was late afternoon. The music was loud, the sweet smell of hickory filled the air and everybody seem to be picking up from last night. Beer and liquor occupied everyone's hand. The strong smell of marijuana engulfed the air and the party started all over again. I knew it would be the last time I would see most of them. I shook off the hangover and decided to have a ball.

I drove home that night from the picnic thinking about the graduation. I knew deep down inside I hadn't done my best in school. My grades should have been a lot better than they were. I was graduating, but I didn't feel like I deserved it. Nor had I earned it. All my life I wanted to be smart like my sister or smarter. I wanted to follow in her footsteps. I knew I had it in me, but, something was always holding me back. I had no idea what it was.

Sunday morning I got up and prepared myself for the graduation. Everybody in my family was proud of me, especially my mother. I wasn't proud of myself. I didn't know what my next move was going to be. I definitely wasn't ready to become a man. My mother had taken care of me my whole life. Now it was time to face the real world and I was scared as hell!

Friends and family flooded the house to congratulate me on a job well done. Coming from a neighborhood like mine, graduating from high school was an accomplishment. I had fought through many adversities to make it thus far. If I wasn't proud of anything, I was satisfied in one area, I had done what my father said I would never do, graduate.

As I walked into the living room, I locked eyes with my father. I had on a two piece dark purple Miami Vice style suit with the purple snake skin shoes. I'm certain part of him wanted to say, "Congratulations son, I'm proud of you." He had been defeated and his pride wouldn't let him speak. I had proven him wrong and I was on my way to my senior graduation. I grabbed my cap and gown and headed for the car. Never looking back for the approval that would never come.

The graduation was packed with proud parents, uncles, aunties, cousins and friends. That year Hyde Park Career Academy graduated four hundred and thirty five seniors. We all walked across the stage with our heads held high. For some of us, life was just beginning. For others, it was just a walk in the park. We were men and women now, ready to make our mark in the world. Yes, the fun was over, it was time to get down to business. I was lost!

Finding Peace

Two weeks after graduation, I had to go pick up my high school diploma from the school. I got up early that morning. I always hated catching the el train to 63rd Street, it was Disciple territory. They loitered around the train station just to catch the Vice Lords coming from the low-end. The train pulled into the 63rd street station and stopped. As I exited the train, I could see opposing gang members lurking in the background of what would soon become a fight for my life.

My first mind told me to get back on the train. I had to get my diploma. Somehow I blended in with the other pedestrians and made it safely across the street to the bus stop. I wasn't out of the water yet. The bus stop was directly across the street from Inglewood High School. It was infested with Disciples. Some of them didn't know me. Most of them did. I didn't make matters any better. It was Friday and I had on all black and gold, Vice Lord colors. I stuck out like a sore thumb.

I stood at the bus stop with my eyes focused on the parking lot at Inglewood High School. The lot was full with disciples and they seemed to all be looking at me. Before I could sort out an escape plan, they entire crowd started to run in my direction. "Vice Lord killer," they yelled. My heart dropped in my shoes. I had nowhere to run, nor did I have a weapon. My life flashed before my eyes. I had to get focused. They wouldn't hesitate to kill me and I knew it. I turned to run. There was no time. My past had caught up with me and suddenly I really needed God.

I found myself in the middle of the gas station parking lot balled up in the fetal position, trying to protect my head. The kicks and punches were coming so fast. I knew I had to get up or die where I lay. I got up and bolted toward the front door of the mini market at the gas station. I flung open the door and locked it behind me. Once inside, I jumped over the counter and demanded to use the phone. Blood was coming from everywhere on my body it seemed. "Give me the freaking phone," I yelled to the cashier. He looked at me as though he hadn't understood a word I said. "Give me the freaking phone," again I yelled. In a split second, he leaped over the counter and unlocked the door. I couldn't believe it, they had members on the inside, damn! There was nowhere to run, I was trapped!

I stood there, petrified! The mob rushed in and grabbed me. The beating started over again. While begging for my life, I heard the sound of a shotgun blast coming from the rear of the store. I remember thinking to myself, "what the f_ _ _ k was that!" It was the store manager. He had heard the disturbance. "Get off him!" he yelled. The cowards raced for the door and scattered in different directions. There was God once again showing up when I hadn't called him.

The manager helped me up. "Do you want me to call police", he asked? Didn't want to involve the police, so, I told him no. He offered to let me use the phone, and I did. Within minutes, the entire corner and gas station parking lot was cluttered with my guys from the hood, including my Father. My father looked at me and I could tell from the expression on his face, I was a total mess. They had broken my nose, two ribs and completely closed up my right eye. As I fell in my father's arms, I noticed the store cashier was still at the register…. And the rest is history.

CHAPTER 14

AFTER A LONG recovery from the beating I took, I decided I needed to do something with my life or die in the streets. My sister was also on my case. I decided to go to school. Columbia College, located downtown Chicago was a logical choice. It was an art school full of students from all around the globe. Attending Columbia was not what I wanted. Once again I found myself trying to please everyone but me.

During this time I had become a party animal. I partied every weekend and soon became a disc jockey with raw skills on the turntables. Columbia College was a school filled with diversity and talent! Some of the most talented artists I ever encountered. Fraternities and sororities engulfed the student lounge everyday competing in step shows. It was hard trying to focus on college at the time because my parents were talking about separating. After being married for forty years, I didn't understand why they couldn't work it out. Even in all that dysfunction, they had always been 'together'. My father was willing, but my mother had finally had enough.

    I spent my entire freshman year isolating myself from other students. I didn't have any friends, nor was I trying to make any. By the time my sophomore year rolled around, I had come out of isolation. I thought making friends would make the college life a little more interesting. As usual, I picked the wrong crowd to hang with. All they did was party! I spent the first half of the year hanging out, partying, and cutting class. My education was going down the drain. I didn't care. I didn't want to be there anyway. I was only doing it to make my family proud.

    Somewhere inside of me was this little voice that kept telling me to change. I was moving too fast. I wanted to do the right thing. It required giving up too much. I didn't understand what serving God really meant. My mother spoke of the Lord God all the time, she prayed consistently. But I watched her suffer and struggle all my life. I saw the blood and tears. I saw her tired and weary body. I saw the stress on her face, and I felt her soul cry out plenty times. Where was God? Why did her prayers seem in vain?

    By the end of my sophomore year, my parents had decided to go their separate ways. It left me torn between the two. I had gotten involved with a young lady from the projects on 53rd and federal. It was my first time experiencing love, so I thought.

    Debra and I had met at my 20th birthday party. I was introduced to her by my best friend, James Taylor. It was one of the biggest mistakes I had ever made when it came to choosing a lady. She was a beautiful brown skinned woman.

She came fully loaded, with a shit load of mental issues that is. I wouldn't find out until later in the relationship just how crazy she was. Once again where was God, why didn't he warn me?

Debra had come into my life at a trying time. My parents were separating and I had just started to experiment with cocaine. The wealthy kids at Columbia had cash and access. When they partied, they partied hard. I was just trying to keep up. Debra was living with her mom in the projects and things were in a uproar there also. Her family lived in the Robert Taylor Homes. The buildings stretched a country mile on State Street. Some of the high rise buildings went as high as the 17th floor. Meeting me was a dream come true for her. She thought I was her ticket out.

After my parents separated, my mother moved to her family home in Mississippi. There was no place for me there. My father moved to Memphis, I went with him.

CHAPTER 15

I'd only been gone a few months when Debra tracked me down. James was dating her sister. He knew where I was and it wasn't long before Debra got the number and address. Surprise! It was about 4 a.m. and I had just got off work. It was the Christmas season. I had landed a job at the Raleigh Springs Mall at Circus World toys. I was sitting on the living room couch when the phone rang. Startled, I grabbed the phone on the first ring. "Hello?" I answered. My father just stood there while my mouth flung open wide enough to catch a swarm of flies.

"Who is it?" finally he asked.

"It's Debra," I said.

"What does she want?" determined he replied.

"She says, she's in Memphis at the bus station and we need to pick her up right now."

My father was never fond of Debra. He agreed we couldn't leave her there stranded.

Finding Peace

When we pulled up in front of the bus station I could see she had picked up a little weight. The closer she got to the car, the more reality kicked in. That extra weight was a baby, she was pregnant.

I will admit, I was glad to see her. She helped me through a really rough time. I wasn't expecting a baby. When I met Debra, she already had a little girl two weeks old. A beautiful ball of joy of whom I had grown very fond of, but this was different. This one was mine and I had no idea how to be a father.

I had grown up with a father who stayed drunk most of time. He never took out the time to teach me about manhood. Most of what I learned, I learned in the streets. Those guys were not men. They were thugs of the worst kind. You didn't model your life after them. You lived your life in fear of them or in spite of them.

The next morning we all got up and ate breakfast. Knowing I was soon to be father would require some changing of plans. I knew she didn't want to live in Memphis. That meant I would be moving back to Chicago. We were only 200 miles from Mississippi. We decided to pay my mom a visit. I had to find out what mom thought about my soon to be new life.

My father, Debra and I arrived in Mississippi about five that evening. I was so glad to see my mother. I didn't even bother talking about her and dad working things out. She seemed to be at peace with the whole ordeal. On the other hand, my father was actually missing her. It showed. In his own way, he loved her deeply and eternally. I came later to understand, he loved her the only way he knew how.

It was always a joy to visit my grandparents as long as I didn't have to stay. My maternal grandparents lived deep in the country. It was so dark at night you couldn't see your hand in front of your face. For entertainment they would assemble themselves on the car porch and tell hank (ghost) stories that would scare us to death as kids. We would spend the whole night under the covers sweating, thinking something bad was gonna happen. My grandfather didn't make matters any better, he would pace the hallways of the house all night. Since it was so dark, all we could hear was footsteps sounding like it was coming straight for our bedroom door. The next morning when the sun rose, we were some happy campers. To kids from the city, Water Valley, Mississippi was a scary place.

After a long talk between my mom, Debra and myself, we convinced my mom to move back to Chicago with us. It was kind of depressing to leave my father behind alone but life had to go on. He had made the bed in which he now had to lay. I needed to get serious about my future and I knew it. It wasn't all about me anymore. I would be a father soon. I was determined not take my child through what I had experienced. We found a two bedroom apartment in the Inglewood neighborhood on the south side of Chicago. In this environment, my problem with drugs started to progress. Real life was stressful. Living with Debra pregnant was a lot harder than I could have imagined. She had mood swings hourly it seemed some days. She and my mom weren't getting along. My money was funny. It was all just too much. I was able to keep it a secret for a while and then things got out of hand. The more stressed I was the more I needed. The more I needed, the MORE I needed. My tolerance increased and so did my dependency. All the things I said I would never do, I did. I was too embarrassed to ask for help. I also didn't think I needed help. Everyone knew I had a problem but me. I had watched plenty of guys in my hood destroy their lives on drugs. Now I was face to face with the same nightmare. But I was in complete control, so I thought.

I remember those long conversations with God staring down the long end of the pipe. Someone I never took the time out to get to know. Now I needed Him in a desperate way. My life was falling apart. I realized I didn't have control anymore. My best thinking almost got me killed more times than I can count. Everybody seem to know what was wrong with me but me. I refused to accept being labeled as "addicted". I got myself in this shit and I will get myself out of it, is what I always said.

The neighborhood we lived in was too risky for me to get comfortable in, it was Disciple territory. My mother was already a nervous wreck. Not knowing what I would do next. I kept her on pins and needles. Finally, she and Debra got fed up with my devious acts and they both moved out. Leaving me to live with my own adversities. Debra took my child and moved back home with her mom. My mother moved in with one of her younger brothers, my uncle JT. I wasn't allowed to visit her while she stayed there. Everybody claimed to be so afraid of me. My aunt had told my mom she didn't want me coming to her house. She went so far as to say if she couldn't keep me from coming, she would have to find somewhere else to stay. I wasn't good at following rules, so I went anyway.

Without my mom, I didn't know the first thing about living on my own. I had been spoiled all my life. I never had to stand on my own. Responsibility was never taught. I always did whatever I wanted to do and no matter what, no one ever spoke against it. I remember thinking about the previous times I thought about what I wanted to be when I grew up. I was young and I had all kinds of dreams. Now the years had flown by so fast. I hadn't met any of my goals, nor was I working at achieving any of them. My parents had broken up and my life suddenly didn't seem worth living.

My mother applied for a job with an agency as a live in house keeper. Shortly after she started with a permanent placement. She moved into a big mansion on Chicago's north shore. Debra and I ironed out our differences and moved back in together. My son was my seed, Derrick Jr. My step daughter was about three at the time. She had become my pride and joy. She was like my own. I had raised her thus far and to her I was daddy. Even though I had a seed of my own, my step daughter Denise had stolen my heart. We spent so much time together she was beginning to look like me. I guess God had it all figured out. He had given me something I never had, responsibility and unconditional love.

Again I found myself in a neighborhood infested with opposing gang members. I didn't have a job at the time. I had children, a woman, and bills! The drug trade was all I had to lean on. I needed to blend in and get paid. I'll never forget the day we moved in. James and I were standing in the front of the building. We were watching everything and everybody that moved. The guys on the block were organized. They had somebody on every corner with two-way walkie-talkies. They yelled out codes that alerted others when the police were in the area. James and I stood there and watched them make at least 2,000 dollars in 1 hour. The block was a gold mine!

I decided I needed a piece of the pie, so, I set up shop. It didn't take long for the money to start rolling in. It was coming so fast, I couldn't keep count! A few months had passed by, and I had blended in perfectly. I kept my tattoos covered so the disciples wouldn't know my true identity. I studied their laws and literature and hired some of their guys.

Everything went smooth the first couple of years. Everybody was making money and they had no clue that I was a vice Lord… and then it happened. One of the chiefs for the Black Stones had gotten out of prison and opened up a drug spot across from where I lived in the same complex. He had been locked up for ten years. Now he was back to claim his territory. I couldn't risk blowing my cover, so, I made a deal with the chief. They called him, "BIG DOC".

Big Doc was a powerful man who demanded a lot of respect. He was making money in Disciple territory and they didn't say a word. After a long sit down, Doc and I agreed to merge in the game. I moved my operation to his spot. We split the shifts into two. He brought in his son, Lil Doc. Lil doc took the first shift from 12 noon to 12 midnight. I took the 12 midnight to 12 noon. The arrangement went well until his son developed a habit and started using the product. After 4 or 5 times coming up short, his father started to ask questions. When he approached me with the situation, I told him the truth. "Your son is using the product."

Doc was a small man about five feet five inches tall, a hundred and thirty pounds soak and wet. But, his reputation in the streets was nothing pleasant. I didn't need the drama, I was in it for the money, and I always knew hustling and gang banging didn't mix. I thought I gained the trust of the Disciples in the hood, but they were planning to rob me and I had no clue. It wasn't me they wanted, it was Big Doc. I was just the bait! The following year all hell broke loose. Big Doc put his son out and gave me control of everything. I stayed up day and night, around the clock chasing money. Counting money and bagging up drugs became my full time job. I was working for the Devil and didn't even know it. Becoming somebody important didn't even matter anymore. I thought I was somebody important. The game had changed me in every area of my character. I became heartless. It was all about the money. Nothing else mattered.

CHAPTER 16

I REMEMBER THE EVENING it all went down............................
I had got up early that morning feeling like something bad was going to happen. God was trying to get my attention, but, I wasn't listening. There were so many signs and I didn't see them. I was sitting in the drug spot looking out the front window when someone knocked on the front door. The knock caught me in a daze and it startled me. "Who is it," I yelled! I stood in front of the door looking through peep hole, it was a customer. After getting rid of the customer, I heard a knock at the back door. It was Lil Doc begging for a bag. I didn't want to give it to him, but, he wouldn't take no for an answer. He got the Bag and left. I locked the bars and sat down at the kitchen table to count the money. After putting everything together, I grabbed the keys and headed downstairs to the first floor to put the count in the safe house. I unlocked the bars

and stepped onto the back porch. Click, click! I remember thinking to myself," that sounds like a gun!"

Suddenly, I felt the cold steel on my neck. "Give us the freaking keys" they yelled! I turned around and swung with all my might, knocking the gunman down the stairs. Before I could gain my composer, they rushed me. There was nothing I could do, I was out numbered. They took the keys from my pocket and opened the door to the safe house. They held me at gun point while they cleaned us out. After they left, I sat there trying to put it all together. I thought to myself, "what am I going to tell Big Doc." I shook it off, locked the door and headed home.

I grabbed the phone and paged Big Doc leaving 911 behind the number. Within seconds, he returned my phone call. "What's up," he asked? "Man I just got robbed, they took everything!" "Who was it," he replied with a strange tone, as though he didn't believe me. "I don't know, it was five of them and they all had on mask." I was lying. I knew exactly who it was, but, I couldn't tell, they had threaten to kill my family. "I'm on my way," he said, and hung up the phone. I looked at Debra and said, "today, I'm going to die!

I didn't know what to do. I didn't have the money to cover what was taken, and I knew Doc wasn't trying to hear nothing I had to say. I told Debra to phone the guys back in my hood and let them know what happened. In the meantime, I prepared myself for the worse.

I sat in the front window watching for Doc's car to pull up. Debra stood behind me begging me not to go. I had to face him. I didn't want him to think I had anything to do with the robbery. About ten minutes had passed by when

Finding Peace

I saw an unfamiliar car pull up in front of the building. Four huge men exited the vehicle dressed in army fatigues. They walked up the walk way and went into the entrance that lead to the drug spot. I had never seen either of the men before. Who could they be, I wondered? A couple of minutes later, Doc pulled up and parked in front of the building. I watched him as he walked down the walk way looking at my front window. He looked pissed off! He stopped in front of my window and waved his hand for me to come out. Something deep inside was telling me not to go. I remembered hearing this same voice speak to me in the past, and I ignored it. Maybe it was God, or maybe it was just plain fear. Whatever it was, I had to go or else I would look guilty. For the first time in my life, I said a silent prayer to myself, asking God to watch over me. I got up, kissed Debra and went to face whatever came my way.

Once I got to the drug spot, I knocked on the door anticipating danger on the other side. "Who is it?" yelled a strong voice from the opposite side of the door. "It's me, Dnice," I replied with a slight tremble in my voice. The door opened and standing in front of me was a huge man dressed in army fatigues holding a sawed off double barrel shotgun. My first mind said, run but my feet wouldn't move. He snatched me in and slammed the door! He stuck the barrel of the shotgun in the center of my back and said, "walk nigga!" It was the longest walk I had ever took in my life. Seconds later, I was standing directly in front of Big Doc! I quickly scanned the room, three other men occupied the room, all holding handguns. I started to explain what happened, and out of nowhere I felt a powerful blow on the top of my head. Immediately, blood spurted from a large hole in the center of my head. Then the beating commenced. I tried to focus, but, I couldn't because of all the blood in my eyes. I crawled to the corner of the room and covered my face the best I could. There was no mercy! Next, they broke my nose, and then my ribs. The beating lasted at least 45 minutes. My body was numb. I prayed for death! gagging on my own blood, I made one last attempt for mercy, and then I lost consciousness.

Somehow, in my unconscious state I could still feel violent assault against my entire body, only it wasn't pain I felt, but, some form of extreme pressure. They were still beating me, and suddenly it was if God had touched me. I opened my eyes. Realizing I was not dead, I pleaded one last time for my life. They sat me up on the couch and asked me for the last time to tell where the drugs and money was. Before I could say a word, Lil Doc knocked at the front door. Doc ordered one of his men to let him in and that took the focus off me. And then the strangest thing happened.... As soon as Lil Doc walked into room, it all came together, He had set me up! I knew never to trust a gangster, and now it might cost me my life.

While his father questioned him about the robbery, I replayed the entire day in my head. The knock at the back door. The bag I gave Lil Doc just before I counted the money to take to the safe house. No one knew about the route to the safe house but, Big Doc, his son and myself. After serving him he went downstairs and told the guys I was about to come out. I trusted him and now his jealousy was about to cost me my life! Finally, I got my chance to tell my story, and it all made sense to Big Doc. They took him out the back door and I never saw him again. I wasn't out of the water yet, I knew too much and there was no way they would let me live.

Doc told them to hog tie me, blind fold me, and duct tape my mouth, put a pillow over my head and blow my brains out. There was no more fight in me, I surrendered my soul to God. They took me to a bedroom in the rear of the apartment, threw me on the bedroom floor and put a pillow over my head. Although I had given up the fight, something inside me refused to give into the reaper. I tried to plead for my life one last time. The duct tape sealed my mouth like a safe. I wiggled and wiggled until the killers became impatient with my noncompliance. "Pick his ass up," one of them yelled! Two of them lifted me from the floor and carried me to the back porch. They took me to the third floor and threw me over the back porch banister. It was the most terrifying thing I had ever experienced. I was falling and there was nothing I could do. I felt the sting of thorns piercing my body as I landed in the bushes below. The bushes had broken my fall. I could hear the pity pat of footsteps running from the third floor, they hadn't finished with me yet.

"This nigga got nine lives," one of them shouted. I laid motionless on the ground below. At first I didn't notice, somehow my hands were free. I pushed myself up on my knees and tore of my t-shirt to wipe some of the blood from my eyes, and there they stood. The man with shotgun, lifted it from his side and aimed it directly at my head. Just as he was about to finish the job one of them yelled, "wait, he's got a hat and cane tattooed on his chest." The tattoo was a symbol that represented Vice Lords. "This nigga is one of ours, we can't kill him," the man with shotgun shouted! "Let's take him back in the house and see what the chief wants to do," another one replied.

God was becoming more real to me, it had to be him. I was God's child and he was protecting me. He had given me a will to fight for my life when I had no will at all. He had cushioned my fall, untied my hands and sat me upright before my executioners. He had softened their hearts and now I would live to see my son grow up. "Thank you Lord," I shouted over and over again while Doc ordered his goons to take me home.

I leaned against the door frame of my apartment while they knocked on my door and left me where I stood. The front door flung open and all I remember is hearing Debra scream. Everything went black. I don't remember much after that. It was six months later before I even knew I was still a part of this cruel world.

CHAPTER 17

AFTER I CAME home from the hospital, it took me a while to focus. I had sustained so much trauma to my head, I was having grand mall seizures every day. I was on three different medications at the same time, all for seizures. The medications eventually started to control the seizures, but the side effects kept me bed ridden. My balance was terrible, I couldn't walk five feet without falling.

Debra was in school at the time, so James came over every day to keep an eye on me. James knew I couldn't continue to live there, and so did I. It wouldn't be long before the disciples knew my true identity, we were sure it all had been revealed after the robbery. While recovering from my injuries, my money got low. I had to do something, and all I knew how to do was hustle. You would think I had learned my lesson after the crazy shit I had experienced. How soon we forget God's blessings. After all he had brought me through, I was still taking him for granted. The disciples got the 411 on me, so, I didn't take any more chances. I moved my family out, and we found an apartment on 81st and Ingleside. We only lived there for a couple of years and then we moved to 54th and Indiana. Our relationship wasn't on the best of terms, so we eventually broke up in 1991. I moved to Lake Forest with my mom and got a chance to experience the life style of the rich and famous. The house was huge! It had four floors, 22 bedrooms, 10 bathrooms, a sun porch, a beautiful Chinese garden that laced each side of the football field length yard and the most breathtaking view you could imagine. But, there was something about that city, I couldn't seem to stay clear of it. I kept going back, finding myself in all sorts of mischief, until I found myself behind bars doing a 18 month sentence. I was released on a five year probation term in 1993. At the time, my brother became terminally ill with cancer of the colon. He was given two to six weeks to live and it was tearing my family apart. He was only forty five years old. The doctors had done all they could do for him and his life ended August 3rd of 1993. I had had enough of Chicago. I moved to Memphis with my father in February of 1994. My life was about to take another roller-coaster ride.

CHAPTER 18

MEMPHIS WASN'T THAT much different from Chicago, just smaller. The city was like a big circle and everybody knew everybody. My father lived in a single family home on Cypress road, the north side of Memphis. His house was at the end of the block next to a huge corn field owned by his brother. Even though it was a city, it still seemed country as hell to me. I was a city boy and where I'm from you didn't see corn fields. I thought to myself, "I'm going to run rings around these country ass nigga's." But, in time they would prove me wrong.

Growing up I never got along with my father's side of the family, they didn't like me. I spent a lot of summer vacations in the south when I was young. My Grandparents were cool, it was my father's brothers I didn't like. They had money and a lot of land. They looked down on poor people. When I arrived in Memphis, my father took me on a tour of the neighborhood. He pointed out all the low lives and the ones who were not worth me meeting.

The neighborhood reminded me of my block back home. Everybody was hanging out. People were all over the streets and every porch had a crowd doing God knows what. After making a few blocks, my father and I finally stop at one of his friend's house. The backyard was full of old men shooting dice and telling old tales of their younger days. There was one tall light skinned woman standing in the mist of the game, she was calling the dice. "Daddy, who is that," I asked with my eyes focused on her well-shaped ass. "That's Millie, the neighborhood drug dealer." A female selling drugs? That's something you didn't see in Chicago.

I had arrived in Memphis at the end of February, and it was already in the seventies. If it was already this live, I wondered what the summer would bring. My Father introduced me to Millie and right away I could tell she was a freak. The first thing she focused on was my midsection. Even though she had a smashing body, I didn't look at her that way. She was a hustler and I knew she would be a benefit to me in the near future. I needed money, and Millie was the source. I hadn't planned on bringing that demon with me. I guess somewhere inside me it hid itself. But, this was a new town, new people, new territory, and no one knew anything about me. I spent the next six months putting together my own mob. The town was full of gangster type men, but, there was no structure. They were unorganized and they lacked proper leadership. I was the new law, it was imbedded in my mind. It was what we lived by in the city. I was supposed to be on a mission for God after all He had done for me.

Finding Peace

I got up early every morning and read the bible faithfully. I tried hard to take in what I read, but, the familiar life style I knew kept resurfacing. All my life people told me God had a purpose for my life. I guess I never took the time to let him order my steps. My disobedience to God's calling was taking me down a road that would all most cost me my life again. Once again, the devil was in the driver's seat. I had formed a mob of dedicated men, but, deep down inside I wasn't sure if I could trust them. I had to remember, I was an outsider, and just like no one knew me, I didn't know anyone either. Since Millie knew everyone, I let her handle most of the business. She was pretty, but, ruthless as hell! She carried a 44 magnum everywhere she went, and she wasn't scared to use it. She had ten children, seven boys and three girls. The three older boys were all gang related. The oldest boy was the real killer in the family. He was feared by many. I knew he would be the one I had to watch the most. He was in jail when I arrived in Memphis, but, people seemed to volunteer information about him. Everywhere I went, he was feared!

I didn't want to be in the spot light, so, I used my barbering skills to keep me busy. I opened up a barbershop in my father's house. While Millie kept the streets in check, I expanded my barbering business and opened up a real barbershop. It was the middle of 1995 and everything was operating smoothly. The barbershop was a success, business was booming. The first year and a half had pasted by so fast, I had forgot to check on my family back home. My brother had died from a progressive stomach cancer in August of 1993. His death left my family scarred for life.

My mother took it real hard, he was only 45 years old, her oldest child. It left his wife and kids emotionally torn. My sister was lost without him, and so was I.

Cutting hair was fine, but, the streets was calling me back, I had to get in the action. I started selling drugs and attending gang meetings. Before long, I found myself residing at the Memphis County Jail for the first time. I had sold drugs to an undercover officer and received a three year sentence. After serving six months at the Shelby County Correctional Center I was paroled on a Friday, January 12, 1996. A day I will never forget. It was the beginning of a weekend that would change my life forever...

I had gotten out about 8 a.m. that morning. It was my first time being incarcerated. When I got home, Millie and I rented a room at the Comfort Inn hotel, I needed to unwind. After some much needed sex, she gave me the 411on what had been going down while I was locked up. I phoned my Mom to let her know I was home. I'll never forget what she said when she picked up the phone... "I need to ask you something," she said. "I need to know if I was a good mother and did I raise you right?" At first the question didn't register. It didn't seem appropriate for the occasion. "Why would she be asking me a question like that," I thought to myself. "Yeah Ma," I replied. "I just needed to know," she said. And then she hung up the phone.

I sat there on the bed, playing that question over and over and over in my head, until finally I fell asleep.

The next morning we got up and checked out of the hotel. Millie dropped me of at my dad's house and she

Finding Peace

went home to begin another day of hustling. Suddenly I felt a need to read God's word. That question my mother had asked me needed God's attention. I grabbed my bible and started reading. I don't remember where I began, I just opened it hoping to find an answer to what I was feeling. Before I knew it, the entire day had past. I had fallen asleep with the word of God clinched tightly against my chest.

That Sunday morning I got up around seven o'clock and started preparing breakfast for my father and I. He was working out in the corn field. I had just about finished when he walked in. "Good morning old man," I said. "The same to ya' son," he replied, sounding nearly out of breath. My father was getting old and I didn't think he needed to be working so hard. But, he was stubborn as hell. He said, if he don't keep busy, he would die, so, I let him be. Just before we sat down to eat, I felt this horrible feeling invade my soul. Something was wrong with my mother, I could feel it. My father noticed it and said, "what's wrong son?" "I don't know pops, I just got this feeling like something has happened to mama." "Give her a call," he said. I picked up the phone and dialed her number.

The Phone seemed to ring forever, and finally someone answered, it was not my mom. "Hello," the strange voice said. "Who is this?" I asked. Now, I knew something was wrong. My mother always answered the phone. "This is the next door neighbor," she said. "Why are you answering my mother's phone, and where is she?" I asked frantically. "She's been rushed to the hospital. I got a call from one your aunts in Chicago and she asked me to come over and check on her. She said, she was talking to your mother and then she heard her drop the phone. When I got here she was lying on the kitchen floor and she wasn't breathing." I dropped the phone. The whole scene seemed like a dream, I just wanted to wake up. Without my mom, I was nothing, and neither was life.

When my father walked in the living room, I was in state of shock! I wanted to call Lake Forest Hospital, but, I was afraid of what I might hear. A few minutes passed by, and I couldn't take not knowing what happened. So, I made the call. "Lake Forest Emergency" the soft spoken woman replied. "Yes, I'm calling to inquire about my mother, her name is Maggie Turner. She was brought in there about an hour ago." "Ah, yes, your family is here. Would you like me to transfer you upstairs to the waiting area?" She transferred the call and my uncle answered the phone. I could tell from the sound of his voice, something was seriously wrong. And then he let it out. "She didn't make it, I'm sorry Derrick."

My whole world was Lost.

CHAPTER 19

THE DAY MY mother died changed my whole life. I was already struggling, trying to find God. Trying to build a relationship with him in my own peculiar way. But, this time he really had turned his back on me, he took the only person I could depend on. The only person who understood me. She spoke highly of God, and now, I was alone in this cruel world with no one to hear my cry. I didn't understand God. He had saved my life numerous of times, and I never heeded to his voice. I spent a great deal of my life running from God. I ignored every opportunity I had to serve him, why was He sparring me? I was so lost when my mother died, I planned to piss God off by making a complete mess of my life. I was a fool to think I was in charge. I was embarking upon the worst ass whipping I would ever get when I made the decision to turn my back on Jesus. It wasn't long before I ended up back in prison for another drug charge, only this time I got three years. Millie was pregnant when I got locked up. It wasn't a question of who the father was, I knew the baby was mine. She was wild but she was faithful. This was the hardest time I ever did. My mother was dead. My best friend was gone forever. I would never hear her voice again, nor would I ever see her smile. Something inside me wanted to call on God. I was so angry at him, my pride wouldn't let me surrender. When I got out, I came home to a beautiful seven pound, ten ounce, baby girl, she was beautiful. She should have been the reason to change my life, but, no. I was on mission for the devil and I knew it. My every action would be in direct disobedience to God!

I hit the streets immediately! I lost the barbershop and the will to even try to redeem it or myself. Death was really what I wanted. I prayed for it every night. I had plenty of time on my hands, and I spent it reorganizing my mob. I jumped right back in the dope game.

The game had changed. The Disciples had took it over and they dared anybody outside their mob to sell a bag. Me, I wasn't easy to scare. Especially by Disciples, I hated them and trouble was just what I was looking for. It wasn't long before I caught another case. This time it was a burglary charge. I did two years on this one and got released in 1999. Millie was tired of me getting locked up. So, I did that bit alone. No visits, no letters and no money orders.

When I got out I got involved with another young lady, her name was Tracie. She was a hood girl, but, I didn't know it at first. I was blinded by her sex appeal. My father saw right through her. He said, "boy you can't turn a [hoe] into a house wife." But, I didn't listen. I was determined to make her mine. After dating about two weeks, we decided to move in together. We found a two bedroom apartment on the north side of Memphis and moved in. Shortly after, I started working at KFC. I tried hard to focus on my new life with Tracie, But, Millie was making it impossible for me to see my daughter. She didn't mind me spending time with her, as long as Tracie wasn't around. So, I went by to spend time with her on my lunch breaks.

Even though I had left the streets alone briefly, I still had a mob to run. My name as the Chief for the Conservative Vice Lords, had become known, and threats were soon flowing all over the town. Tracie had gotten pregnant and we were expecting a baby girl. After the baby was born, our relationship went downhill. I was working most of the time, and the rest was devoted to the mob. They protected me and my family. Then the threats got worse. I had caught another charge for possession of a controlled substance and bonded out the next day. Since, I was out on bond fighting another case, I stayed in the back ground as much as possible. I had established a reputation that the Disciples didn't agree with. I had taken the threats too lightly, and before I knew it I found myself bound to a wheelchair from the destruction of 13 bullets. The bullets had damaged my right leg and lower spine, I couldn't walk. I was getting just what I deserved, turning my back on Jesus. The near death experience I had in Chicago should have opened my eyes, but, it didn't. Now that my mother was gone, I really didn't care if I lived or died.

I plead guilty to the charge I was fighting and got three years. But, there was something different about this bit Once I was on the inside I felt a different feeling. A feeling

I had not felt before. Or maybe it was a familiar feeling, but, this time I heeded to it. Yes, change was necessary, and change had to happen. I needed to know God. I wanted to know God. There had to be someone who loved me more than my mother in spite of all my short comings. Someone kept sparring my life, and I had to know who.

I spent my time getting familiar with Islam. It was a fast growing faith in the prison system. I read the Holy Quran faithfully and in no time, I was saying my prayers in Arabic. I attended service every Wednesday and Friday, but, something wasn't right. It seemed like I wasn't serving the right God. The more I studied, the more I noticed they didn't know Jesus, and it scared the hell out of me. To them he was only a man, but, to me he was the Son of God.

Before long, I started attending the Christian service. As soon as I walked in the chapel I felt God open up his arms and received me. I knew then, I was in the right place. I went to therapy every day, praying that God would let me walk again, and he did!

In prison there is two kind of men, those who serve God and those who serve the devil. For once in my life, I had chosen to serve God. A couple of months before my release, my father passed away from a stroke. Now, both my parents were deceased. This time I didn't blame God. I had learned the hard way, He is in charge.

CHAPTER 20

AFTER I GOT out my legs were still weak. I was on a walker for a while. I had nothing else to remain in Memphis for. I had burned my bridges with Millie, and Tracie had gone her way. I prepared myself to move back to Chicago. Moving back to Chicago wasn't what I wanted to do, but, I had nowhere else to go. At least I would be on familiar turf. I knew the city like the back of my own hand. This time I needed to make the right choices. My life had been down some dead end roads, but, this time would be different. It had to be! Or I would die for sure.

I hated to leave my girls behind, but, I had to move on. I caught the bus July 3rd 2003. During the ride I had time to reflect on my mistakes. I had made many in my life. It was time to grow up! Mama wasn't there to bail me out anymore, and neither was my father. When I got here I moved in with my nephew and his wife. He had become a man. He had established a family of his own and seemed to be doing well for himself. My nephew's wife was mean as hell! My past life brought about trust issues and she didn't want me there. The situation was putting my nephew in a bad position. My nephew lived on the southwest side. Once again I found myself right smack in the middle of Disciple territory. How the hell did I keep moving in the wrong neighborhood, I don't know. Even though my nephew was a Disciple, it wouldn't do me much good to hide behind his status, he didn't associate with the ones on his street.

After a week passed by, I started getting out a little; trying to get a feel of the neighborhood. I made sure I kept my tattoos hid, I would be stupid not to. Thugs were all over the block. Some gang banging and others we're selling drugs. It was mid-summer and all types of criminal activity was going on. I was trying to keep my focus on Jesus, but, I wasn't strong enough yet. I was paying too much attention to the negativity that surrounded me.

The first person I met was a gay girl name Vicky. She was about 28 years old. Vicky was a beautiful light skinned woman. Why she was attracted to the same sex was beyond my comprehension. All I could do was look at her and say to myself, "what a waste." Vicky lived on the third floor of an apartment building with her girlfriend. They had turned the apartment into a drug spot. People knocked on the door all night long, looking for crack and Vicky had plenty.

I knew it was a bad move for me. A drug house rolling like this, it was only a matter of time before the place got raided.

The apartment was like prison, bars everywhere. I guess it was necessary, but, I didn't like it. It reminded me to much of the life I wanted to leave behind. I was tired of the streets, but, I had attached myself to them and now I needed to find a way out. I fought it hard to stay straight. I had let the gang banging go. The hustle wouldn't leave me alone. At the blink of an eye, I was wrapped in the same self-destruction. "Damn," I thought to myself. But, this time it was different. I felt an over whelming guilt engulf me. God was convicting every evil thought.

After my mother died, everybody sort of went their own way. It was like we all became instant strangers. Nobody kept in touch anymore, I hated what had become of my family. Everybody was blaming everybody, but no one looked at themselves. My mother, brother and my father had worked hard to build a family and now it seemed to be all in vain. Now they were looking down on us at what a mess we have made of everything they built.

Even though 63rd was new turf for me, it didn't take me long to blend in. I met all the wrong people it seemed, almost overnight. Hanging out, selling drugs and getting high became my everyday routine. Bad decisions became the norm. I had rekindled the fire and before long, I would be doing my first prison term in Illinois. Things started to heat up at my nephew's house, I needed somewhere to go. I tried to stay out of the house as much as possible to keep down the confusion. But, that didn't work. I was up to my old ways again and my nephew's wife wasn't having it.

I ended up moving in with Vicky and her girlfriend, another bad choice I made. Since all of the bedrooms in the apartment were occupied, I made a bedroom out of the enclosed back porch. At least this way I could see the police if they tried to come in through the back. I spent my mornings just sitting out in front of the building watching the activity on the block. Even though I was new in the area, no one seemed to be paying me any attention, so I thought. Someone had saw one of my tattoos and the word was out. I was sitting in front of the building one morning like I did every morning, and three guys walked up to me. "What's up my nigga," one of the young guys said? I didn't have a response, I knew it wasn't the welcoming committee. I got up and turned to walk back in the building when I felt the blow of a blunt object strike me on the back of my head. The force from the blow knocked me clear into the hallway! Before I could get to my feet, all three of them smothered me with punches, kicking me and stomping me without any consideration for my life. They left me in hallway unconscious. When I regained consciousness, I was in the back of an ambulance, being rushed to Holy Cross Hospital.

No matter how hard I tried, I couldn't seem to stay out of harms way. I spent the next six years in and out of prison. My children were growing up without a father, and I didn't know why God was allowing me to suffer.

CHAPTER 21

THE END OF 2009 was the year I saw my salvation………
The streets had beaten me down for the last time!
It was a bitter cold day in December. I was standing in front of the 7Eleven food and liquor store about 9:30 p.m. when I heard the voice of God. "It's time my child," He said. "Come to me all who are heavy laden and I will give you rest." It was the most heartfelt thing that had ever happened to me, instantly I felt his presence. A peace that surpasses all understanding, fell over me. I remember feeling a joy that brought tears to my eyes. But, this time the tears weren't tears of sorrow or self-pity. They were tears of joy! I knew in that moment God had saved me. All I needed to do was surrender, and I did! My life was about to change for real this time, and I would let nothing turn me around. The devil was and still is a lie!

That night I left 63rd street. I caught the bus downtown to the Pacific Garden Mission, a shelter for the homeless. But, God had other plans for my life. The shelter had a men's bible institute on campus. He was ordering my steps and for the first time, I was letting him. I enrolled in bible college the second day I was there. It took a couple of months for me to settle in, I still hadn't got all that stubbornness out of me, I was a mess and I knew it wasn't going to happen overnight. Besides, everybody wasn't in school to change their lives. Some were there just for the privileges the school had to offer. Those were the ones the devil had placed there to be stumbling blocks for those like myself who were truly seeking God. Once I learned how to put on the whole armor of God, I was well on my way.

I studied my bible all the time, and the more I studied, the more of Himself he revealed to me. My thoughts started changing. My attitude adjusted. My decisions got better, and my choices improved my life. God was giving the increase, and I loved every second of it!

I prayed each night with a sincere heart. Thanking God for all he had done for me and all he had yet to do. He had brought me threw a whirlwind of sin, and I was forever grateful. What I had longed for was finally mine, a peace of mind.

After Bible College, I caught up with my best friend James Taylor. He had moved out in Hickory Hills, a suburb just outside of Chicago. James and I had been best friends since my sophomore year in high school. At the time, I had a three month lease at The Crossroads Hotel on 53rd and Pulaski. When the lease was up, I moved to Hickory Hills to stay with James and his fiance, Lisa.

Hickory Hills was just what I needed to stay focused. It was quiet and laid back. The complex we lived in had a lake in the back with ducks and geese gliding gracefully across the smooth settled water. The neighbors were friendly and the air smelled of fresh cut grass. I continued studying my bible and praying every night faithfully. I watched the neighbors go to and fro, attending bible study, choir practice and church every week. It was what I always wanted deep down inside, a relationship with God. All I needed was a church home, and God would soon bring it to pass.

Finally my mind was at peace, I could think clearly. I could feel the Holy Spirit working inside me. God was restoring me. Every morning I got up and took walks around the lake, thinking about how far I'd come. Thinking about all the people I had hurt. Thinking about how much I hurt myself. I thought about how God must have felt to see His son suffer on the cross, and it hit me! I was his child too. How bad had I hurt God?

During these walks, God would talk to me. "Stop beating yourself up," a still voice inside me would say. "I have forgiven you of all your sins, so go ye therefore and tell the world of my mercy and grace." Each Sunday I watched my upstairs neighbor leave with her children, headed for church. I could feel her spirit as she walked past my living room window. I wanted what she had. She was dedicated.

One morning I caught her on her balcony studying God's word. It was the first time I saw her that close. She was beautiful. Her face had a glow. I could see the spirit working in her life. I grabbed a chair and sat down outside my front door. I looked up at her and locked my eyes on her until she noticed me. "Good morning," I said, with a pleasant voice. When she turned to lock eye's with me, instantly I knew she was what I had been praying for. "Good morning," she replied, with the most beautiful smile I had ever seen. Her voice was soft and seducing. Her eyes were glossy and glittery like the sun reflecting off a hill of diamonds. Only if my mom were alive, I knew what she would say, "that's the one son, go for it!"

I invited her downstairs and asked if we could study together and she said, "yes." We sat there for hours, reading the bible and exchanging a little information about ourselves. You noticed I said, "a little information." There would be so much more to learn about this mysterious woman in the near future. As the days came to pass, I found myself spending all my time with her. I was falling in love with a total stranger. We took walks around The lake together every evening when she got off work. We shared our past Relationships and talked about what we expected in the next one. We both had experienced some heart breaking moments, and now we longed for Happiness.

Every night we shared milk shakes from McDonalds. We sat in the Parking lot in her car and talked about our future together, or at least I did. Yvette was shy. All she did was look at me and smile. I spent a lot of time at her apartment. We cuddled on the living room couch and watched movies all night. She always fell asleep first. I watched her sleep, she was beautiful, and with any luck, she would soon be all mine. As time went on, Yvette and I fell in love. Finally, God had blessed me with the perfect woman. I stayed at her house every night. She wouldn't let me go home, and I didn't want to.

Our bond became inseparable. We both dived into our new life together, head first. It wasn't long after that when she started questioning me about my walk with God. It was uncomfortable at first. I knew a lot about God, But, I didn't have a personal relationship with Him, or at least not the kind of relationship I wanted. Her belief was strong and so was mine. We spent a lot of time debating scripture. I still had a lot of growing to do In the word, and I thought I knew it all. Yvette opened my eyes to a lot about my study of the bible. She saw things different, but I must admit it lined up with the text. Our relationship was moving fast! Within a couple of months, I moved in with her. We were both struggling at the time, so, we didn't have much. She was starting over and so was I. At first, we didn't realize how far of the mark we were. God was convicting us. Suddenly, everything I did or thought of that didn't line up with the word of God, brought about an unbelievable guilt. I felt compelled to change, it seemed necessary. All the wrong I'd done seem to flood my conscience at once! How far I'd come, didn't matter anymore. What I was going to do with rest of my life was now my first priority. Yvette and I had been dating for about seven months. She had three beautiful girls I had grown very fond of. Our relationship was growing, but, there was something missing. We didn't have a real commitment, at least not the kind God required. We were having sex and we were not married. If we had any intention of doing the right thing, and we did, we would have to get married. There was no doubt in my mind, I loved her and I wanted to spend the rest of my life with her.

Finally, I stuck my chest out and popped the big Question, I asked her to marry me and she said yes!

We didn't have a big wedding, we got married downtown. It was one of the most soul fulfilling moment I ever had. On the way home I couldn't stop looking at her, she was all mine and I was the proudest man alive. I had tried to get married in the past, but, none measured up to what God had blessed me with. Yvette was the perfect catch and I knew it! In the beginning the kids didn't approve of me. They did everything in their power to tear us apart, it was hell! The whole house was against what I was trying to build. The devil was at work again, causing all sorts of confusion, and then her son came home from jail. He had been locked up for 6 months. Somewhere down through the years she had lost control of him. He started to get in all kinds of trouble. When he got out of jail he was only 16, but, he was a hand full. He reminded me so much of myself, smart and very talented, but, his head was hard as a brick! Datren was his name. He was an intelligent bright young growing man with plenty of potential. He grew up with no father figure and he had held that resentment in his heart for years. He challenged me in every area he could think of, but, I held my position as a father. I shared with him my faults and my experiences. I told him all about my walk on the dark side. I knew what it was like to lose control of self. What it was like to want to do the right thing and couldn't. He was struggling with that same demon and I knew God had placed him in my life for a reason. I needed to reach him. I needed to find a way to assure him that God loved him and He wanted only the best for his life! Yvette raised him in the church, but, he had lost his way. As parents we were so busy into ourselves, we had forgotten how important it was to lead by example.

My plans to let God direct my life were failing. My wife had fallen away from the church. It seemed as though the devil was doing what he does best, destroy! The struggle with Datren was becoming impossible to endure. I wanted to give up on him, but, something inside me warranted me to demonstrate Love at all costs. I watched my wife's heart bleed for his salvation, and all I could do was join her in the fight.

CHAPTER 22

THE FIRST YEAR of my marriage was challenging. The fiery darts of the wicked invaded my new life with Yvette from all angles. It seemed as though everybody wanted to see our marriage fail. When I look back on the Word of God, I'm reminded of Ephesians chapter 6:10-19; "finally, my brethren, be strong in the Lord and in the power of his might; Put on the whole armor of God, that Ye may be able to stand against the wiles of the devil. For we wrestle not against flesh and blood, but against principalities, against powers, against the rulers of the darkness of this world, against spiritual wickedness in high places. Wherefore take unto you the whole armor of God, that ye may be able to withstand in the evil day, and having done all, to stand. Stand therefore, having your loins girt about With truth, and having on the breastplate of righteousness; And your feet shod With the preparation of the gospel of peace; Above all, taking the shield of Faith, wherewith ye shall be able to quench all the fiery darts of the wicked. And take the helmet of Salvation, and the Sword of the spirit, which is the word of God: Praying always with all prayer and supplication in the Spirit, and watching thereunto with all perseverance and supplication for all saints; And for me, that utterance be given unto me, that I may open my mouth boldly, to make known the mystery of the gospel." Knowing God's word was one thing, but, applying it was the hard part.

I was married now and I had to be a man, there were no more excuses! God had given me a title, head of the household. Responsibility came with being A Christian and I was ready! Being a Christian meant letting go of the world and I had suffered enough. I expected everything to change overnight, but it didn't work that way. I had been living in sin all my life and there was some things I had to pay for. God began to test my faith. He blessed me and he punished me. He allowed me to be tempted. Sometimes I passed the test and sometimes I failed. The road was getting rough and there were times I thought my marriage was in Jeopardy. We were verbally attacking one another all the time. It took a while before we realized it was only the enemy trying to tear down what God had joined together.

The one thing I loved about my wife was, she never stayed mad long. She had a unique way of letting go of useless baggage. As for me, I still had a long way to go before I reached that level, and somehow I knew Yvette would help me get there. She was a piece of work! I watched her all the time. I wanted what she had, but, I knew it hadn't come easy. A lot of pain came with the faith she possessed.

Somehow, despite her adversities, she always found time to let go and let God.

As time went on, we learned together how to smooth out the rough Places. We learned how to respect each other's opinions about different things. But, most of all, we learned how to turn it all over to God. I'm not saying life became a bowl of cherries, but, at least we had a Savior name Jesus who could do all things. He had been given all power in heaven and in earth and that was the best news any sinner could hope for.

God began to restore all that the devil had stolen from both of us. Most of all he restored our peace and mind. He showed us how to focus on him. Before long, Yvette and I got back in church. She was already a member at New Memorial Baptist Church on the south side. After attending a few services, I found my home there too. New Memorial is a Christ centered church with a heart and not an attitude, and you could feel the love when you walked through the door. They embraced me with open arms! Now all I had to do was open my heart and receive what God had for me, and boy was I ever so ready! Things are different now. God has given my life purpose. Being a part of the church family is awesome! Coming together every Sunday to worship God is amazing and I love it! He saw the best in me even when I thought there was no repentance.

Looking back on all I endured in my life, sometimes gives me the chills. The trials and tribulations of life taught me, that sin will take you further than you want to go, keep you longer than you want stay and cost you more than you are willing to pay. I won't say I have regrets. Even though the roads got rough, I learned a great deal about survival and how to defeat my adversary, the devil. I learned no matter what I faced, God was able to see me through! The devil had defeated me, but, Jesus had defeated him, and because of his love for me, I became a new creature. I gave my life to Christ and he wiped away all my sins. He hung on a rugged cross, stretched his Arms wide and died for me. But, early one Sunday morning, he got up with all power in His hands, and for that I am forever grateful.

For all of you who have endured some challenges in life and you feel like giving up, don't, you can do all things through Christ who strengthens you. All things work together for the good to them that love God, and are called according To his purpose. God's will for us is that all be saved, and that none shall perish in the pits of hell. He continues to give us what we don't deserve, and we continue to put him to an open shame! Think about it. What have you done today to please God first? Do we seek him daily? Do we praise him only in time of need? Are we living the way God instructed us to live? Jesus said, "He has prepared a place for us, that where he is, we may be also." We should not only be thankful for what God has done, but, we should be living everyday with our eyes on the prize!

If you have not given your life to Jesus, I strongly suggest you try Him, he's waiting to change your heart. He changed mine and I love him for his Marvelous work I pray that all mankind come to know the risen savior. He has waited with unbelievable patients. It's time we all surrender our hearts to our creator.

www.ingramcontent.com/pod-product-compliance
Lightning Source LLC
LaVergne TN
LVHW091604060526
838200LV00036B/993